I0696823

HOW TO MAKE MONEY IN STOCKS

A-Z STEPS TO BECOME A PRO IN INVESTMENT (ULTIMATE GUIDE)

By

MIKE HERTZOG

All rights reserved. No part of this publication may be reproduced, distributed, or transmitted in any form or by any means, including photocopying, recording, or other electronic or mechanical methods, without the prior written permission of the publisher, except in the case of brief quotations embodied in critical reviews and certain other noncommercial uses permitted by copyright law.

Copyright © MIKE HERTZOG 2024.

TABLE OF CONTENTS:

INTRODUCTION TO THE STOCK MARKET

You could see a news title that says the securities exchange has moved lower, or that the securities exchange shut up or down for the afternoon. Most frequently, this implies financial exchange files have gone up or down, meaning the stocks inside the record have either acquired or lost esteem all in all. Financial backers who trade stocks desire to make money through this development in stock costs.

HOW THE MARKET FUNCTIONS

At the point when you buy a public organization's stock, you're buying a little piece of that organization.

The securities exchange deals with an organization of trades — you might have known about the New York Stock Trade or the Nasdaq. Organizations list portions of their stock on a trade through an interaction called a first sale of stock, or Initial public offering. Financial backers buy those offers, which permits the organization to fund-raise to develop its business. Financial backers can then trade these stocks among themselves.

Purchasers offer a "bid," or the most noteworthy sum they're willing to pay, which is normally lower than the sum dealers "inquire" for in return. This distinction is known as the bid-ask spread. For an exchange to happen, a purchaser needs to build his cost or a vendor needs to diminish hers.

This all might sound muddled, however, PC calculations by and large truly do most cost-setting computations. While purchasing stock, you'll see the bid, ask, and bid-ask spread on your dealer's site, yet generally speaking, the distinction will be pennies, and will not be of much worry for novice and long-haul financial backers.

Chapter 1

All things considered, stock trades most likely happened in a genuine business place. These days, the monetary trade works electronically, through the web and online stockbrokers. Each trade happens on a stock-by-stock reason, but stock expenses, all things considered, habitually move pair considering data, political events, monetary reports, and various factors.

Keep in mind, that there are no ensures in the financial exchange, and past execution isn't demonstrative of future outcomes. Continuously be wary and settle on informed choices in light of your monetary circumstances and objectives.

WHAT IS THE SECURITIES EXCHANGE DOING TODAY?

Financial backers frequently track the securities exchange's presentation by taking a gander at an expansive market record like the S&P 500 or the DJIA. The outline underneath shows the ongoing presentation of the financial exchange — as estimated by the S&P 500's end cost on the latest exchange day — as well as the S&P 500's authentic exhibition starting around 1990.

WHAT IS A MARKET?

A market is where gatherings can accumulate to work with the trading of labor and products. The gatherings included are normally purchasers and merchants. The market might be physical, similar to a retail outlet, where individuals meet up close and personal, or virtual, similar to an internet-based market, where there is no actual presence or contact among purchasers and vendors.

A few key qualities assist with characterizing a market, including the accessibility of a field, purchasers, and dealers, and an item that can be bought and sold.

FEATURED DISCUSSIONS ABOUT MARKET

A market is where purchasers and vendors can meet to work with the trade or exchange of labor and products.

Markets can be physical, similar to a retail outlet, or virtual, similar to an e-retailer.

Models incorporate unlawful business sectors, closeout markets, and monetary business sectors.

Markets lay out the costs of labor, not entirely set in stone by the organic market.

Highlights of a market incorporate the accessibility of a field, purchasers and dealers, and awareness.

HOW MARKETS FUNCTIONS

A market is where at least two gatherings can meet to participate in a monetary exchange — even those that don't include legitimate delicate. A market exchange might incorporate merchandise, administrations, data, cash, or any mix that passes starting with one party and then onto the next. To put it plainly, markets are fields in which purchasers and vendors can accumulate and communicate.

Two gatherings are by and large expected to make an exchange. Nonetheless, an outsider is expected to present a contest and equilibrium in the market. Thus, a market in a condition of wonderful contest, in addition to other things, is described by countless dynamic purchasers and dealers.

Past this wide definition, the term market envelops different things, contingent upon the unique situation. For example, it might allude to the financial exchange, which is where protections are exchanged. It might likewise portray an assortment of individuals who wish to purchase a particular item or administration in a specific spot, for example, the Brooklyn real estate market. On the other hand, it could allude to an industry or business area, for example, the worldwide jewel market.

Certain choices assist with molding the still up in the air by a monetary framework known as the market economy. In this framework, factors like speculations and the creation, circulation, and estimating of labor and products are driven by organic markets from organizations and people. In that capacity, a market economy is spontaneous and isn't important for an arranged or ordered economy where the public authority directs these elements. Instances of market economies incorporate the US, Canada, the Assembled Realm, and Japan.

Chapter 2

WHAT ARE STOCKS

HOW DO STOCKS FUNCTION?

A stock addresses an offer in the responsibility for the organization, remembering a case for the organization's profit and resources. In that capacity, investors are halfway proprietors of the organization. At the point when the worth of the business rises or falls, so does the worth of the stock.

Stocks are by and large traded electronically through stock trades, the two essential ones in the US being the New York Stock Trade (NYSE) and the

Public Relationship of Protections Vendors (NASDAQ). While certain organizations sell stock straightforwardly to financial backers, most just sell stock through a financier like Schwab.

Financial backers trade stocks for various reasons including the possibility to develop the worth of their speculation over the long haul, to possibly benefit from more limited-term stock value moves, or even to procure a pay by putting resources into profit-paying stocks. The thinking behind these choices is frequently derived from subjective and quantitative procedures like a central examination or specialized investigation. Remember that the cost of a stock can fall as effectively as it can rise. Putting resources into stock offers no assurance that you will bring in cash, and numerous financial backers lose cash all things considered. Installment of stock profits isn't ensured, and profits might be suspended. The hidden normal stock is liable to market and business gambles including bankruptcy.

RESOURCES AND MARKETS

A Prologue to the Securities Exchange

Understanding the securities exchange is vital for pursuing informed exchange choices. You want to know how to pick the right stocks, which requires an inside and out comprehension of an organization's yearly report and fiscal summaries. Figure out how to comprehend what stock addresses in an organization and how to decide the genuine worth of any stock. This permits you to settle on better money management choices by staying away from the expensive slip-up of buying an organization's stock when the market has pushed its portion cost excessively high compared with its worth.

ESSENTIAL REALITIES

To turn into a fruitful financial backer, you should comprehend the securities exchange and how organizations issue stock.

Organizations that need to develop past more modest, mother-and-pop tasks might decide to open up to the world, offering part of the business to financial backers.

At the point when organizations choose to give stock, they approach guarantors, for example, Goldman Sachs or JP Morgan, which decide the worth of the business.

The financial exchange capabilities as a huge closeout where possession in organizations is offered to the most elevated bidder every day.

FINANCIAL EXCHANGE TERMS

The initial step to understanding the financial exchange is knowing the language. The following are a couple of normally utilized words and expressions:

__INCOME PER OFFER__: The all-out organization benefit isolated by the quantity of stock offers extraordinary.

__OPENING UP TO THE WORLD__: Shoptalk for when an organization intends to have an Initial public offering of its stock.

__INITIAL PUBLIC OFFERING__: Another way to say "first sale of stock," is when an organization sells its portions of stock interestingly.

MARKET CAP: Another way to say "market capitalization," is how much cash you would need to pay if you somehow managed to purchase every portion of stock in an organization. To ascertain market cap, duplicate the quantity of offers by the cost per share.

SHARE: An offer, or a solitary normal stock, addresses one unit of a financial backer's proprietorship in a portion of the benefits, misfortunes, and resources of an organization. An organization makes shares when it cuts itself into pieces and offers them to financial backers in return for cash.

TICKER IMAGE: A short gathering of letters that addresses a specific stock as recorded on the securities exchange. For instance, The Coca-Cola Organization has a ticker image of KO, and Johnson and Johnson has a ticker image of JNJ.

GUARANTOR: The monetary establishment or venture bank that does the desk work and coordinates an organization's all's Initial public offering.

PROLOGUE TO THE FINANCIAL EXCHANGE

The functions of the financial exchange can befuddled. Certain individuals honestly think financial planning is a type of betting and feel that assuming you contribute, you will probably wind up losing your cash.

These apprehensions can come from the individual encounters of relatives and companions who have faced the same outcomes or survived the Economic crisis of the early 20s. These sentiments are reasonable yet aren't grounded in reality. Somebody who has faith in this logic might not have that frame of mind about the securities exchange, why it exists, and how it works.

CONTRIBUTING BY FOLLOWING THE GROUP

Others accept that they ought to contribute for the long run yet don't have the foggiest idea where to start. Before finding out about how the securities exchange functions, they see effective financial planning as some kind of sorcery that a couple of individuals know how to utilize. As a rule, they surrender their monetary choices to experts and can't explain to you why they own a specific stock or common asset.

This speculation style could be called ignorant religiosity, or maybe it's restricted to a feeling, for example, "This stock is going up — we ought to get it." However it may not appear to be so by all accounts, this gathering is in definitely more peril than the first. They will quite often contribute by following the majority and afterward can't help thinking about why they just accomplish fair, or, now and again, decimating results.

FIGURING OUT HOW TO CONTRIBUTE

After learning a couple of procedures, the typical financial backer can assess the monetary record of an organization and, following a couple of somewhat straightforward estimations, show up with their understanding of the genuine worth of an organization and its stock.

This training permits a financial backer to take a gander at a stock and realize that it is worth, for example, $40 per share. It allows every financial backer to decide when the market has underestimated stocks, expanding their drawn-out returns significantly, or exaggerated them, making them unfortunate speculation competitors.

Chapter 3

WHY DO COMPANIES SELL STOCK?

While figuring out how to esteem an organization, it assists with grasping the idea of a business and the financial exchange. Pretty much every huge organization began as a little, mother-and-pop activity and, through development, turned into a monetary goliath.

The Requirement for Subsidizing

As an organization develops, it keeps on confronting the obstacle of collecting sufficient cash to subsidize progressing extension. Proprietors by and large have two choices to defeat this test: They can either get the cash from a bank or financial speculator, or they can offer a piece of the business to financial backers and utilize the cash to support development. Organizations frequently take out a bank credit, since it's ordinarily simple to get and extremely valuable, to a certain degree.

Banks will not necessarily loan cash to organizations, and over-excited chiefs might attempt to get excessively, which adds a ton of obligation to an organization's monetary record and damages its exhibition measurements. Factors, for example, frequently rouse more modest, developing organizations to give stock. In return for surrendering a minuscule part of possession control, they get money to extend the business.

Opening up to the world gives an organization cash that doesn't need to be repaid. It likewise gives the business directors and proprietors another device. Rather than paying money for specific exchanges, for example, the obtaining of another organization or business line, they can utilize their stock.

HOW IS STOCK GIVEN?

To all the more likely comprehend how giving stock functions, take the imaginary organization ABC Furniture, Inc. In the wake of getting hitched, a youthful couple chose to begin a business. This permits them to work independently and orchestrate their functioning hours around their loved ones. Both a couple have consistently had serious areas of strength in furnishings, so they choose to open a store in their old neighborhood.

After getting cash from the bank, they named their organization ABC Furniture, Inc. furthermore, started a new business. During the initial not many years, the organization creates little gain, because the profit once again into the store, purchasing extra stock, redesigning, and growing the structure to oblige the rising degree of product.

GOING WITH THE CHOICE TO SELL OFFERS

After a decade, the business has developed quickly. Two or three have figured out how to take care of the organization's obligation, and the benefits are more than $500,000 each year. Persuaded that ABC Furniture could do too in a few bigger adjoining urban communities, the couple chooses to open two new branches.

They research their choices and figure out that they need more than $4 million to extend. Not having any desire to get cash and make obligation and premium installments once more, they choose to raise assets by offering value to likely investors, so they sell stock in their organization.

TRACKING DOWN A GUARANTOR

The organization moves toward a guarantor for the stock contribution, for example, Goldman Sachs or JP Morgan, which dives into their fiscal reports and decides the worth of the business. As referenced previously, ABC Furniture acquires $500,000 in after-charge benefits every year. It likewise has a book worth $3 million, which incorporates the worth of the land, building, stock, and different resources, in the wake of covering the organization's obligation. The guarantor investigates and finds that the typical furniture stock exchanges are available at multiple times its organization's profit.

What's the significance here? Just expressed, you would duplicate the organization's income of $500,000 by 20.

For ABC's situation, that outcome is a market-esteem assessment of $10 million. Assuming you include the organization's book esteem, you show up at $13 million. This implies, from the financier's viewpoint, that ABC Furniture has an all-out worth of $13 million.

CHOOSING THE AMOUNT OF THEIR BUSINESS TO SELL

The youthful couple, presently in their 30s, should conclude the amount of the organization they will sell. At this moment, they own 100 percent of the business. The more organization shares they sell, the more money they'll raise, however, they should remember that by selling more, they'll be surrendering a bigger piece of their possession. As the organization develops, that possession will be worth more, so a savvy business visionary wouldn't sell more than the individual in question needs to.

In the wake of talking about it, the couple chooses to stay with 60% of the and sell the other 40% to people in general as stock. At the point when you crunch the numbers, this implies that they will keep $7.8 million worth of the business (60% of the $13 million worth). Since they own a larger part of the stock, more noteworthy than half, they will in any case be in charge of the store.

The other 40% of their desired stock to offer to people in general has a worth of $5.2 million. The guarantor finds financial backers who need to purchase the stock and gives a check for $5.2 million to the couple.

Even though they own less of the organization, the proprietors' stake will ideally develop quicker since they possess the ability to quickly grow. Utilizing the cash from their public contribution, ABC Furniture effectively opened two new stores and has $1.2 million in real money left more than since it raised $5.2 million however just utilized $4 million.

UTILIZING THE PAY TO EXTEND AND DEVELOP

Their business performs stunningly better in the new branches. The two new stores each make around $800,000 a year in benefits, while the old store makes the equivalent of $500,000. Among the three stores, ABC currently creates a yearly gain of $2.1 million.

Even though it no longer has the adaptability of a private venture or the opportunity to just close shop, its organization is currently esteemed at $51 million. You would arrive at this figure by increasing the net profit of $2.1 million every year by 20 (the typical furniture stock referenced before) and adding the organization's most recent book worth $9 million since each store has a book worth $3 million. The couple's 60% stake presently has a complete worth of $30.6 million.

THE ADVANTAGES OF SELLING AND CLAIMING OFFERS

With this model, it's not difficult to perceive how private ventures appear to detonate in esteem when they open up to the world. The first proprietors of the organization, one might say, become richer short term. Previously, the sum they could remove from the business was restricted to the benefit that was produced. Presently, they can sell their portions in the organization whenever raising money rapidly.

This cycle frames the premise of Money Road. The securities exchange capabilities as an enormous sale where proprietorship in organizations very much like ABC Furniture is offered to the most elevated bidder every day. Due to human instinct and feelings of dread and eagerness, an organization can sell for definitely more or undeniably not exactly its characteristic worth. A decent financial backer figures out how to recognize those organizations that are as of now selling beneath their actual worth so they can purchase whatever number offers as would be prudent.

Chapter 4

CLASSES OF STOCKS

Before you buy stock or issue stock as a feature of another organization, you want to have a comprehension of the fundamental classes of stock. Each class of stock accompanies its bundle of highlights (casting ballot rights, cost, payout need, and so on), bringing about various benefits and detriments related to each. Here is a look.

WHAT ARE CLASSES OF STOCK?

In the most broad terms, there are two primary kinds of stock: normal and liked. In any case, each sort of stock might be additionally recognized by class.

Note: "Classes of stock" ought not to be mistaken for "classes of offers." Albeit the two terms might be tradable while alluding to organization stock, the expression "classes of offers" may likewise allude to various classes of common asset shares.

WHY ARE CLASSES OF STOCK SIGNIFICANT?

The various classes of stock are taken care of in an unexpected way, especially with regards to casting a ballot rights, and the need for delivering resources and profits. Assuming you are an investor, hence, the sorts and classes of stocks that you own will affect your portfolio's general worth. If you are a new company, the sorts and classes of stock you issue might influence how much stock you sell and the general valuation of your business.

NORMAL STOCK

Normal stock is suitably named since it is the most normal sort of stock given by an organization. By and large, on the off chance that you buy stock in an organization on a significant trade, you will purchase normal portions of stock. Normal stock investors have casting ballot rights that permit them to choose individuals from the top managerial staff and give a voice in organization strategies.

They likewise have a possession stake in the organization and a case to a portion of the organization's benefits. On the off chance that the organization has likewise given favored stock, normal investors are set in an optional position while partaking in the organization's resources (i.e., after obligation holders and favored investors) in case of liquidation or Chapter 11.

Normal stock possession might accompany other vested privileges, like precautionary freedoms (the option to keep up with relative proprietorship in the organization on the occasion more stock offers are given.)

CLASSES OF NORMAL STOCK

For most organizations giving house stock, there may be one class of that normal stock, with each offer giving equivalent valuation and freedoms to every other offer. There are organizations, nonetheless, that issue at least two classes of normal stock. These various classes are generally assigned by letter (Class A, Class B, Class C, and so forth.).

The main motivation for giving various classes of normal stock is to take into account the task of more prominent democratic privileges (known as "super-casting a ballot" rights) for one class over another. For instance, an organization might make one class of stock (Class A), to be claimed by the organization pioneers and senior leaders just, that doles out a more prominent per-share casting a ballot "numerous" than one more class of normal stock (Class B). Now and again, that numerous might be essentially as high as multiple times that of the organization's Class B normal stock, implying that each portion of Class A stock accompanies 10 votes, contrasted with one decision in favor of each Class B share. The motivation behind doing this is to guarantee that the pioneers and leaders keep up with command over the organization's directorate and major corporate choices. In this specific model,

Class An offers wouldn't be publically exchanged, their accessibility restricted rather to organization originators and senior leaders.

This is one more illustration of the way an organization might structure various classes of normal stock:

Class A - Class An offers are like the offers given by an organization with only one normal stock class. That is, Class An offers are accessible to individual financial backers and the public. Each offer accompanies one vote.

Class B - Class B shares are like those portrayed in the primary model as Class An offers. That is, they are not accessible for exchange to individual financial backers and are restricted to proprietorship by organization pioneers and top chiefs. Per-share casting a ballot power might be a numerous of those Class An offers.

Class C - Class C offers are like Class An offers in all perspectives, then again, actually the Class C offers need casting ballot rights.

As should be visible from the two models introduced here, there are no terms or arrangements intended for specific class assignments. The standards and elements of various stock classes rely on how every particular organization characterizes them. For instance, a few organizations assign less democratic power to their Group A stock, when contrasted with Class B stock, trying to mask this weakness to people in general. Subsequently, it is essential to constantly cautiously check the insights about an organization's stock classes to decide precisely the exact thing that is being presented with each class.

Class D Stock - Class D stock is a typical stock assignment that has as of late been involved by various organizations for shares accessible just to organization pioneers. Class F imparts normally come to highlights, for example, super-casting ballot rights and limitations on open exchanging.

FAVORED STOCK -

Favored stock is the other significant sort of stock given by organizations. Likewise with normal stock, favored stock investors have a possession stake in the organization and a case to a portion of the organization benefits. They likewise normally get profits in a decent sum on their favored offers and partake in vital position (over normal investors) to organization resources in case of the organization's liquidation or Chapter 11. Then again, responsibility for stock does exclude casting a ballot rights. Favored stock is now and then portrayed as giving highlights of the two bonds and normal stock offers. Favored stock can be grouped by the accompanying four sorts:

Combined stock permits investors to persist in missed profit installments on the off chance that the organization quits delivering those profits and, starts paying them once more.

NoNon-aggregate-tock doesn't permit proprietors to gather profits that might have been skipped.

Taking part stock could have higher profit installments, as long as the organization has bigger than-anticipated benefits.

Convertible stock might be changed over completely to a specific number of normal stock offers.

CLASSES OF FAVORED STOCK

Separate classes are ordinarily an element of normal stock. Be that as it may, organizations can give various classes of favored stock. The various classes are regularly recognized by each other by the need for an installment of profits and circulation of resources upon organization liquidation or Chapter 11.

Assuming that you conclude you want assistance with figuring out which stock to purchase or how to allot stock for your beginning up, post your inquiries on UpCounsel's commercial center. UpCounsel screens out 95% of legal counselors to give you replies from the best attorneys. UpCounsel's lawyers have a normal 14 years of training experience each.

Chapter 5

HOW STOCKS CONNECT WITH THE MARKET

Stocks connect with the market through their worth and execution. The securities exchange is where stocks are traded, and their still up in the air by the organic market of financial backers. The general exhibition of the financial exchange is much of the time seen as a sign of the general soundness of the economy, and stocks can be influenced by variables like monetary circumstances, organization execution, and international occasions.

The exhibition of individual stocks can likewise affect the more extensive market, as well as the presentation of explicit areas or ventures. For instance, on the off chance that a huge organization's stock cost drops fundamentally, it can affect the general market. On the other hand, if an area or industry encounters solid development, it can lift the whole market.

In general, the connection between stocks and the market is mind-boggling and interconnected, with both affecting and being impacted by one another.

ESSENTIAL TIPS FOR EXACT SPECULATION

Putting resources into stocks can be a method for bringing in strong cash, yet it implies risk. Here are a few fundamental stages:

SELF INSTRUCTION: Find out about securities exchanges, fiscal reports, and venture procedures.

PUTTING FORTH MONETARY OBJECTIVES: Characterize your goals and the sum you're willing to contribute.

MAKING A BROADENED PORTFOLIO: Spread your ventures across various stocks to decrease risk.

STOCKS EXPLORATION INVESTIGATION: Dissect organizations before effective money management, taking into account their monetary well-being and development possibilities.

REMAIN INFORMED: Stay aware of market patterns, monetary news, and company refreshes.

RISK THE EXECUTIVES: Just contribute what you can bear to lose, and consider setting stop-misfortune orders.

LONG HAUL APPROACH: Investing is much of the time more effective when finished with a drawn-out viewpoint.

USING INVESTMENT FUNDS: Open a record with a dependable financier stage to work with exchanges.

ROUTINELY SURVEY PORTFOLIO: Evaluate and change your portfolio in light of changing economic situations.

KEEP IN MIND, look for exhortation from monetary experts, and think about your gamble resistance before settling on speculation choices.

ESSENTIAL EXCHANGING SYSTEMS IN THE STOCK TRADE MARKET

PATTERN FOLLOWING: Trade in light of the overall market pattern. For instance, purchase stocks in an upturn and sell in a downtrend.

SWING EXCHANGING: Exploit short to medium-term cost developments. Merchants mean to catch "swings" inside a laid-out pattern.

DAY EXCHANGING: Execute exchanges inside a solitary exchanging day, exploiting intraday cost variances. Positions are shut before the market closes.

FORCE EXCHANGING: Spotlight on stocks' serious areas of strength for execution, guessing that patterns will proceed. This procedure includes recognizing and riding force.

ESTEEM EFFECTIVE MONEY MANAGEMENT: Put resources into underestimated stocks, depending on the major investigation. The objective is to purchase stocks beneath their characteristic worth.

Antagonist Contributing: Conflict with the predominant market feeling. Purchase when others are selling, and sell when others are purchasing, in light of the conviction that markets go overboard.

EXCHANGE: Exploit value contrasts of similar resources in various business sectors. Brokers purchase low in one market and sell high in one more to create a gain.

MATCHES EXCHANGING: At the same time trade two related stocks to benefit from their relative exhibition. The methodology intends to benefit from the difference/intermingling of the two stocks.

BREAKOUT EXCHANGING: Distinguish key help or obstruction levels and exchange when the cost gets through these levels, demonstrating a potential pattern continuation.

SCALPING: Make little, fast exchanges to profit by insignificant cost changes. Hawkers go for the gold on a solitary day, depending on little cost developments.

Keep in mind, that every procedure has its dangers, and achievement frequently relies upon economic situations, risk resilience, and careful examination. It's pivotal to remain informed and adjust techniques on a case-by-case basis.

All in all, the financial exchange is a complicated environment impacted by different variables. Financial backers take part in trading stocks to gain market elements. Effective interest requires grasping organization execution, financial markets, and financial backer feelings. The inborn instability and eccentrics make it urgent for financial backers to lead careful exploration and remain informed to pursue informed choices. While the financial exchange offers potential open doors for development, it likewise conveys chances, underlining the significance of a very educated and vital methodology.

THE URGE TO INVESTMENT IS A GOOD THING. LEARNING TO INVEST IN STOCKS IS ENTIRELY DIFFERENT. AS THERE ARE RISKS INVOLVED IN INVESTMENT, TAKING THE NECESSARY BOLD STEPS MAKES IT VERY EAZY AND STRESS FREE.

Don't invest in any platform you're not sure of. Be wise and endeavor to invest what you can afford to loose. As the Success in Stock investment are not fully guaranteed.

www.ingramcontent.com/pod-product-compliance
Lightning Source LLC
Chambersburg PA
CBHW050047260726
48658CB00005B/1825